tastes of
CHINA

JACKI PASSMORE

WELDON
PUBLISHING
SYDNEY · HONG KONG · CHICAGO · LONDON

A Kevin Weldon Production

Published by Weldon Publishing
a division of Kevin Weldon & Associates Pty Limited
372 Eastern Valley Way, Willoughby, NSW 2068, Australia

First published 1991
Reprinted 1992
© Copyright: Kevin Weldon & Associates Pty Limited 1991
© Copyright design: Kevin Weldon & Associates Pty Limited 1991

Printed in Singapore by Kyodo Printing Co (S'pore) Pte Ltd

National Library of Australia Cataloguing-in-Publication data

Passmore, Jacki.
  Tastes of China.

  Includes index.
  ISBN 1 86302 121 3.

  1. Cookery, Chinese. I. Title. (Series :
  Tastes of Asia).

641.5951

Cover photograph: A selection of Dim Sum.

Frontispiece: A selection of Dim Sum (recipes pages 4–7).

Opposite title page: Eggplant Sichuan Style, and Ma Po Beancurd (recipes page 35).

CONTENTS

APPETISERS

SPICY PORK BUNS

Dough:
750 g (1½ lb) plain flour
125 g (¼ lb) sugar
1 tablespoon baking powder
2 tablespoons melted lard
¾ cup water

Filling:
500 g (1 oz) Chinese roast pork
1 cup water
1 teaspoon cornflour
3 teaspoons potato flour (or extra cornflour)
3 teaspoons dark soy sauce
1 tablespoon oyster sauce
pinch of salt
1½ tablespoons sugar
2 cloves garlic, minced
2 spring onions, minced
30 g (1 oz) pork fat, diced
2 tablespoons oil

Sieve flour into a basin and add sugar and baking powder. Make a well in the centre and pour in melted lard. Mix lightly into the flour, then add water and work to a smooth dough. Knead for 8 minutes, then cover with a damp cloth and leave to rise for 30 minutes.

Slice roast pork then cut into small pieces. Put into a saucepan with all filling ingredients except spring onions, pork fat and oil and simmer on low heat for 10 minutes.

Steam pork fat for 10 minutes, and add to the roast pork mixture with spring onions. Fry the mixture in oil on moderate heat for 2 minutes.

Roll the dough out into a long sausage and cut off pieces about 5 cm (2 inches) long. Flatten with the fingers and fill with a spoonful of the mixture. Pull the dough up around the filling and twist the joins to seal well. Put a piece of plain paper on the joined part of each bun and place paper-side down in a steamer. Cover and leave to rise for a further 10 minutes, then steam over high heat for 20-25 minutes. Serve hot in the steaming baskets.

STEAMED SPINACH DUMPLINGS

Makes 30.

Pastry:
125 g (¼ lb) plain flour
⅓-½ cup boiling water
2 tablespoons sesame oil

Filling:
155 g (5 oz) spinach
2 tablespoons sesame oil
1 teaspoon salt
½ teaspoon sugar
¼ teaspoon white pepper
1 teaspoon dark soy sauce

Sieve flour into a mixing bowl and make a well in the centre. Pour in boiling water and stir with a wooden spoon until all water is incorporated. Leave to cool slightly, then transfer to a floured board and knead for 12 minutes until soft and pliable. The more time spent in kneading, the thinner the pastry can be rolled. Cover pastry ball with a damp cloth and set aside.

Wash and dry spinach and chop very finely. Add seasoning ingredients and mix thoroughly.

Roll pastry into a long sausage about 4 cm (1½ inches) in diameter. Cut slices about 0.5 cm (¼ inch) thick. Roll each out very thinly into a circle. Brush one side with sesame oil and place a small mound of the spinach filling in the centre. Fold into a crescent, and press edges together and pinch to seal. Arrange on a piece of greaseproof paper in a steamer and cook over rapidly boiling water for 20 minutes.

PRAWN DUMPLINGS

HAR GOW

Makes 30.

Pastry:
See Steamed Spinach Dumplings

Filling:
100 g (3½ oz) raw prawns or shrimp
30 g (1 oz) canned water chestnuts
1 small onion
1 clove garlic (optional)
2 teaspoons oil
1 teaspoon soy sauce
½ teaspoon salt
pinch of white pepper
2 egg whites
cornflour
1 egg, beaten

Prepare wrapper pastry and set aside. Mince prawns and water chestnuts. Mince onion with garlic and fry in oil for about 2 minutes until soft. Allow to cool, then mix with prawn and water chestnut paste and season with soy sauce, salt and white pepper. Bind with egg whites and a little cornflour.

Roll out pastry into thin rounds and place a spoonful of the prawn paste on each. Fold over to form crescent shapes and pinch edges together. Seal with a little beaten egg. Place on a piece of greaseproof paper in a bamboo steamer and steam over rapidly boiling water for 15 minutes. Serve hot.

MEAT DUMPLINGS
SHAO MAI

Makes 24.

Pastry:
1 package frozen or fresh *shao mai* wrappers
Filling:
2 large leaves Chinese cabbage
45 g (1½ oz) canned bamboo shoots
60 g (2 oz) lean pork
2½ teaspoons light soy sauce
pinch of salt
white pepper
pinch of sugar
2 teaspoons cornflour
fresh coriander leaves, finely chopped
crab roe, crumbled

Leave pastry to thaw. Wash cabbage and bamboo shoots and chop very finely. Mince pork and mix with cabbage, bamboo shoots, soy sauce, Chinese wine, salt, pepper and sugar. Bind with cornflour.
  Place a spoonful of filling in the centre of each *shao mai* wrapper then gather the sides of the wrapper up to form into a small cup shape. The top should be open. Crimp at the sides to form a slight 'waist' and flatten bottoms to stand upright. Decorate the tops with a little chopped coriander and crab roe. Place in a steamer on a sheet of oiled greaseproof paper and steam over rapidly boiling water for 25 minutes.

COLD CHICKEN WITH SESAME AND MUSTARD SAUCES

500 g (1 lb) cooked chicken breast
90 g (3 oz) processed jelly fish or vermicelli sheets
2 tablespoons sesame paste
2 teaspoons sesame oil
lemon juice or white vinegar
sugar
salt
2 tablespoons hot mustard powder
3 teaspoons oil
3 teaspoons chilli oil (optional)
3 spring onions, shredded

Slice chicken thinly, then cut into shreds. Shred jelly fish (if used) and drop into boiling water to soften. It may be necessary to boil it briefly to soften, but this will depend on the type used. Soak vermicelli sheets in warm water until softened. Drain well and shred.
  Mix sesame paste with sesame oil and add lemon juice or vinegar, sugar and salt to taste. Blend in enough water to make a reasonably thin sauce. Mix mustard with oil and water to make a second thin sauce.
  Arrange jelly fish or shredded vermicelli on a serving dish and pile the chicken on top. Sprinkle with chilli oil (if used) and shredded spring onions. Pour on the two sauces or serve them separately in small jugs.

ASSORTED MEAT PLATTER

8 thin slices braised beef steak
8 thin slices Chinese roast pork
8 thin slices pressed boiled pork or sausage
90 g (3 oz) boiled chicken, shredded
90 g (3 oz) braised chicken livers, thinly sliced
90 g (3 oz) jelly fish or vermicelli sheets, soaked and
    shredded
10 spears canned asparagus
salt and pepper powder
sweet bean paste or plum sauce

Arrange the meat and liver in a pattern around a serving dish. Place two spears of asparagus between each different lot of meat. Sprinkle shredded jelly fish or vermicelli with sesame oil and pile into the centre.

Serve with dips of salt and pepper powder and sweet bean paste or plum sauce.

MEATBALLS ON SPINACH

Makes 24.

500 g (1 lb) beef steak
45 g (1½ oz) pork fat
2 spring onions
4 sprigs fresh coriander
½ teaspoon grated lemon rind
2 teaspoons salt
2 tablespoons dark soy sauce
pinch of white pepper
1½ teaspoons sesame oil
1 teaspoon bicarbonate of soda
3 tablespoons cornflour
3 tablespoons water
24 spinach leaves
2 tablespoons vegetable oil

Mince beef finely with pork fat, spring onions and coriander. Blend in lemon rind, salt, soy sauce, pepper, sesame oil and baking soda and work to a smooth paste. Add cornflour and water and knead until smooth. Form into 24 balls. Leave for 15 minutes.

Wash spinach leaves and arrange on a fireproof plate. Sprinkle on half the oil and place meatballs on top. Sprinkle with remaining oil and place over a steamer to cook for about 12 minutes. Serve with hot mustard.

SPRING ROLLS

Makes 12.

1 packet large spring roll wrappers
oil for deep frying

Filling:
8 dried Chinese mushrooms, soaked
120 g (4 oz) minced pork
2 tablespoons oil
6 canned water chestnuts, chopped
1 tablespoon finely chopped fresh coriander leaves
4 spring onions, minced
1 clove garlic, crushed (optional)
30 g (1 oz) canned bamboo shoots, finely chopped
45 g (1½ oz) beanshoots
45 g (1½ oz) small cooked shrimp
1½ tablespoons dark soy sauce
1 teaspoon sugar
3 teaspoons cornflour
½ teaspoon salt

Separate the spring roll wrappers and cover with a cloth until needed. Squeeze water from the mushrooms and shred finely. Stir-fry the minced pork and mushrooms in 2 tablespoons oil for 1½ minutes; add the water chestnuts, coriander, onions, garlic and bamboo shoots and stir-fry for another 1½ minutes; then add the remaining ingredients and stir-fry for 1 minute. Remove and leave to cool.

To fill spring rolls, place a portion of the filling in the centre of a wrapper. Fold one corner over and squeeze the filling into the required shape. Turn two sides over the roll and then roll up towards the end point. Moisten the end with cold water to stick down.

Heat oil for deep frying. Fry several spring rolls at a time until golden. Drain on absorbent paper and serve hot with soy or sweet and sour sauce (see page 16, Sweet and Sour Prawns).

GREEN ONION PASTRIES

Makes 6.

500 g (1 lb) plain flour
¾ cup boiling water
cold water as needed
3 teaspoons salt
1 tablespoon oil
1½ tablespoons sesame oil
20 spring onions
oil for shallow frying

Sieve flour into mixing bowl and make a well in the centre. Pour in boiling water and mix with a wooden spoon until blended as much as possible. Leave to cool, then gradually work in cold water to make a firm dough which should be neither dry nor sticky. Add salt and knead for 3 minutes. Cover with a damp cloth and let stand for 10 minutes, then knead for a futher 3 minutes.

Roll pastry out to about 0.5 cm (¼ inch) thickness and cut into six rectangles. Brush one side with a mixture of oil and sesame oil. Finely chop spring onions and scatter over the cakes. Fold the pieces over to make a tube shape, then twist into a round cake. Roll out flat.

Heat a little oil in a large frying pan and put in several cakes. Cover and cook on moderate heat until golden brown underneath. Turn and cook other side. Shake pan sharply several times during cooking to make the cakes puff up slightly. Remove from the pan, drain and wrap in a cloth until ready to serve. Cut into quarters and serve on a warmed plate.

STEAMED HONEY SPONGE

30 g (1 oz) honey
185 g (6 oz) butter
100 g (3½ oz) sugar
5 eggs
1 cup fresh milk
375 g (¾ lb) plain flour
2 teaspoons baking powder

Mix honey with butter, then blend in a quarter of the sugar. Beat until light and smooth. Separate eggs. Beat yolks into butter mixture gradually with remaining sugar. Beat until smooth. Add milk and sift on flour with baking powder. Fold in. Leave to stand for 15 minutes.

Whip egg whites until fairly stiff and fold into the mixture. Line the bottom of a baking tin with greaseproof paper and grease lightly. Line the sides with thin cardboard to aid steam in reaching all around the cake evenly. Pour in batter and steam over rapidly boiling water for 40 minutes. Serve warm or cold.

SEAFOOD

SWEET AND SOUR FISH FINGERS

375 g (¾ lb) thick fish fillets
½ teaspoon salt
pinch white pepper
1 teaspoon ginger wine (see glossary)
2 teaspoons cornflour
1 teaspoon sesame oil
125 g (¼ lb) plain flour
60 g (2 oz) cornflour
2 teaspoons baking powder
2 teaspoons oil
oil for deep frying

Sauce:
½ cup white vinegar
75 g (2½ oz) brown sugar
1 tablespoon tomato paste
1 tablespoon dark soy sauce
¾ cup light chicken stock
2 teaspoons cornflour
4 drops red food colouring
pinch of salt
1 cm (½ inch) piece fresh ginger, shredded
2 cloves garlic (optional)
2 spring onions
½ small carrot
15 g (½ oz) canned bamboo shoot
1 small fresh red chilli
30 g (1 oz) celery

Cut fish into pieces about 10 cm by 2.5 cm (4 inches by 1 inch) and dry with kitchen paper. Sprinkle with salt, pepper, ginger wine, cornflour and sesame oil and leave to marinate for 10 minutes.

Prepare sauce by mixing ingredients from vinegar to salt in a small saucepan. Add shredded ginger. Chop garlic and spring onions finely and add to the pan. Scrape and shred carrot, drain and shred bamboo shoot, slice chilli and shred celery. Add all vegetables to the pan. Bring to the boil, stirring until the mixture clears and thickens. Boil for 4 minutes. Keep hot until needed.

Make a batter with plain flour, cornflour, baking powder, oil and enough water to make a batter of dropping consistency. Heat oil until smoking hot. Lower heat to medium. Dip fish into the batter and fry until cooked. Drain and place on a serving dish.

Serve the sauce separately, or pour over the fish pieces just before serving.

FISH WITH HOT BEAN SAUCE

1 whole bream, snapper, or golden carp, weighing
   500 g (1 lb)
oil
1 cm (½ inch) piece fresh ginger
2 cloves garlic
2 tablespoons light soy sauce
1 ½ tablespoons hot bean paste, or *hoisin* sauce
1 tablespoon Chinese wine
2 teaspoons sugar
½ cup water
cornflour
2 teaspoons Chinese brown vinegar or lemon juice
1 teaspoon sesame oil
spring onion, chopped

Clean and scale fish and make several deep diagonal
cuts across each side. Heat 5 cm (2 inches) oil in a *wok*
and fry fish for 1 minute on each side. Lift out and keep
warm.

Chop ginger and garlic finely. Pour out all but 1
tablespoon oil. Fry ginger and garlic for 2 minutes, then
stir in soy sauce, bean paste or *hoisin* sauce, wine and
sugar. Cook for 1 minute, then add water and bring to
the boil. Return fish to the pan and simmer on moderate heat until fish is done. Turn once during cooking.

Carefully lift fish onto a serving dish. If necessary
thicken sauce with a little cornflour mixed with cold
water. Spoon sauce over the fish and sprinkle with
brown vinegar or lemon juice and sesame oil just before
serving. Garnish with chopped spring onion.

STEAMED WHOLE FISH WITH GINGER AND GREEN ONION

1 whole bream or perch weighing 500 g (1 lb)
1 ½ teaspoons Chinese rice wine
½ teaspoon salt
¼ teaspoon white pepper
6 spring onions
4 cm (1½ inch) piece fresh ginger, shredded
1 ½ teaspoons oil
2 teaspoons light soy sauce
sprigs of fresh coriander

Clean fish, removing scales and intestines. Rinse well,
wipe dry, then make several deep diagonal cuts across
each side. Sprinkle on Chinese wine and stand for 10
minutes. Rub fish with salt and pepper and put on a
lightly oiled plate. Shred spring onions and place half
inside the fish together with half of the ginger. Scatter
remaining onion and ginger onto the fish. Sprinkle on
oil and soy sauce and a very little water.

Cover and cook over high heat in a steamer for about
10 minutes until fish is tender. Test if the fish is done
by piercing the thickest part with a thin skewer. If the
flesh appears slightly flaky and no pink liquid runs out
the fish is done. Do not overcook. Lift onto a serving
plate, pour on the cooking liquid and garnish with
fresh coriander.

STUFFED CRAB CLAWS

12 crab pincers with meat intact
375 g (¾ lb) raw shrimp, peeled
100 g (3½ oz) fresh breadcrumbs
1 teaspoon salt
¼ teaspoon white pepper
3 teaspoons lemon juice
½ teaspoon dry mustard
2 egg whites
2 eggs, beaten
cornflour
white sesame seeds
oil for deep frying
12 small lettuce leaves
tomato slices

Break shell away from meat on pincers leaving meat attached to the claw. (It will cling to the central sinew.) Pound shrimp meat to a paste and add fresh breadcrumbs, adding a little water if the mixture is too dry. Season with salt, pepper, lemon juice and mustard and bind with egg whites. Press mixture around the crab meat to form a smooth ball with the claw tip exposed. Coat very lightly with cornflour, then brush with beaten egg. Dip the end of each ball into toasted sesame seeds, coating thickly. Coat again with cornflour.

Heat oil and fry several claws at a time for about 2½ minutes until golden brown. Drain well. Place lettuce on a serving plate and put a crab claw in the curl of each leaf. Decorate the plate with sliced tomato.

ABALONE IN OYSTER SAUCE

375 g (¾ lb) canned abalone
12 lettuce leaves
2 tablespoons oil
2 teaspoons sesame oil
⅓ cup chicken stock
2 teaspoons Chinese rice wine
1 tablespoon dark soy sauce
3 tablespoons oyster sauce
sugar
white pepper
cornflour

Drain abalone and cut into thin slices. Drop into a saucepan of boiling, slightly salted water and simmer for 2 minutes. Drain well. Drop lettuce into a pot of boiling water to which 1 tablespoon oil has been added. Remove at once and drain well. Arrange on a serving plate and sprinkle with sesame oil and remaining oil.

Bring remaining ingredients from chicken stock to oyster sauce to boil and season to taste with sugar and white pepper. Thicken with a little cornflour mixed with cold water if necessary. Put in abalone and simmer for 2 minutes, then spoon onto the lettuce and serve hot.

12   *Opposite: Steamed Whole Fish with Ginger and Green Onion, and Sweet and Sour Fish Fingers (recipes pages 10 and 11).*
Overleaf: Stir-fried Shrimp on Crisp Rice (recipe page 15).

FISH SERVED IN TWO WAYS

1 whole garoupa, snapper or golden carp, weighing
  1–1½ kg (2–3 lb)

1:
2 tablespoons light soy sauce
1 tablespoon rice wine, ginger wine or dry sherry
½ teaspoon sesame oil
1 tablespoon finely shredded ginger
2 spring onions, trimmed and shredded

2:
cornflour
oil for deep frying
2 tablespoons oil
½ small green pepper, finely chopped
½ fresh red chilli or red pepper, finely chopped
2 teaspoons minced fresh ginger
½ clove garlic, crushed (optional)
1 spring onion, minced
½ teaspoon white pepper
1 teaspoon salt
1½ tablespoons white vinegar
2 tablespoons sugar
2 tablespoons tomato ketchup
½ cup water
1 teaspoon cornflour

Remove one fillet from the fish. Cut crossways into
thick slices and set aside.

Place the remaining fish on a heatproof plate. Splash
on the soy sauce, wine and sesame oil, and sprinkle the
ginger and onion on too. Set in a steamer and cook
over simmering water for about 8 minutes or until
tender.

Coat the sliced fillet with cornflour and deep-fry in
the oil until golden and almost cooked through.
Remove to a rack covered with absorbent paper.

Saute pepper, chilli, ginger, garlic and spring onion
in 2 tablespoons oil until softened (about 2 minutes).
Add the remaining ingredients, mixed together in a
small dish, and stir until the sauce boils and thickens.

Reheat the deep-frying oil, and fry the fillet briefly
a second time to crisp the surface. Pour on the sauce
and serve at once. Serve the steamed fish on a separate
plate.

STIR-FRIED SHRIMP IN HOT SAUCE

375 g (¾ lb) raw shrimp, peeled
3 teaspoons rice wine, ginger wine or dry sherry
1 teaspoon salt
2 egg whites, well beaten
½ cup cornflour
oil for deep frying

Sauce:
4 spring onions, trimmed and minced
1 cm (½ in) piece fresh ginger, shredded
4 cloves garlic, crushed
2 tablespoons oil
1 teaspoon sesame oil
1–2 tablespoons chilli bean sauce (to taste)
1–2 teaspoons sugar
2 teaspoons cornflour
¾ cup stock

Season the shrimp with the wine and salt and set aside for a few minutes. Make a batter of the egg whites and cornflour, adding a little cold water. Coat the prawns and deep-fry in hot oil until crisp and golden. Remove and drain on absorbent paper.
 Stir-fry the onions, ginger and garlic in the oil for about 1 minute. Add the sesame oil, bean sauce and sugar. Cook briefly. Stir cornflour into the stock, add to the pan and bring to the boil. Simmer until thickened. Adjust seasonings to taste. Add the shrimp, toss quickly in the sauce and serve at once.

FRIED SHRIMP BALLS

375 g (¾ lb) raw shrimp, peeled
½ teaspoon salt
30 g (1 oz) pork fat, steamed
2 teaspoons Chinese rice wine
1 teaspoon sesame oil
2 egg whites
1 tablespoon cornflour
¼ teaspoon white pepper
oil for deep frying
sweet soy sauce or *hoisin* sauce

Smash shrimps with the side of a cleaver until reduced to a smooth pulp. Add salt and very finely diced pork fat. Work in remaining ingredients except for oil and sweet soy sauce and knead until smooth and well mixed.
 Heat oil to smoking point. To make shrimp balls squeeze a ball of the paste from clenched fist out between thumb and forefinger. Scoop off with a spoon and drop into the oil. Deep fry until golden and crisp on the surface. Lift out and drain.
 Serve with a dip of sweet soy sauce or *hoisin* sauce.

STIR-FRIED SHRIMP ON CRISP RICE

2 cups cooked short-grain white rice
375 g (¾ lb) raw shrimp, peeled
1 teaspoon rice wine, ginger wine or dry sherry
2 teaspoons cornflour
½ teaspoon salt
1 egg white, beaten
oil for deep frying
2 cups fish stock, or stock made from shrimp shells and
  heads
2 teaspoons tomato paste
1 tablespoon chilli bean sauce (mashed)
sugar to taste
60 g (2 oz) frozen green peas
1 small carrot, diced
1 medium onion, diced
cornflour

Press the rice into an oiled oven tray and place in a low
oven overnight until well dried out. Cut or break into
squares.

Season the shrimp with wine, cornflour, salt and egg
white, and set aside for 20 minutes. Deep-fry in the oil
until they change colour. Remove and keep warm.

Bring the stock to the boil; then add the remaining
ingredients except the cornflour and simmer for about
6 minutes, until the vegetables are tender. Mix cornflour with a little cold water and stir into the sauce.

Heat the deep-frying oil and fry the rice cakes until
crisp and golden. Drain and place in a dish.

Add shrimp to the sauce and pour over the rice at
the table. Serve immediately.

LOBSTER WITH SALTED BLACK BEANS AND CHILLI

750 g (1½ lb) fresh lobster
2 teaspoons rice wine, ginger wine or dry sherry
3 teaspoons salted black beans
2 cloves garlic
1 teaspoon sugar
1–2 fresh red chillies, thinly sliced
1 cm (½ inch) piece fresh ginger, shredded
3 spring onions, trimmed and cut into 2.5 cm (1 inch)
  pieces
3 tablespoons oil
½ cup chicken stock
oil for deep frying
cornflour

Cut the lobster open along both sides of the tail.
Extract the tail meat in one piece. Clean the head.
Rinse the tail shell thoroughly and drain. Set aside.
Slice the tail meat and season with wine. Set aside.

Finely chop the black beans and mix with garlic and
sugar. Stir-fry chillies, ginger and onion in 3 tablespoons oil until the onion softens. Add the black bean
mixture and cook briefly.

Coat the lobster pieces very lightly with cornflour
and deep-fry in oil until the surface is sealed. Remove
with a slotted spoon and toss with the ingredients in
the other pan. Add the stock mixed with 1 teaspoon
cornflour and cook until the sauce thickens.

Coat the lobster head and shell with cornflour and
deep-fry until reddened. Drain and place on a serving
plate surrounded by shredded lettuce. Pile the lobster
meat into the upturned tail shell and serve.

SWEET AND SOUR PRAWNS

12 large raw prawns
½ cup cornflour
2 egg whites, very well beaten
oil for deep frying

Sauce:
¼ cup white vinegar
75 g (2½ oz) sugar
2 tablespoons tomato ketchup
⅓ cup water or light stock
2 teaspoons cornflour
½ teaspoon salt
2.5 cm (1 inch) piece fresh ginger, shredded
2 spring onions, shredded
30 g (1 oz) Chinese mixed pickles, shredded

Prepare the sauce first. Mix vinegar, sugar, tomato ketchup, water or stock in a saucepan with the corn-flour and salt. Bring to the boil and simmer for 2 minutes. Add the remaining ingredients and simmer gently while the prawns are cooking.

Peel and devein prawns. Coat lightly with cornflour and dip into beaten egg white. Coat with cornflour again, shaking off excess. Heat oil and deep-fry prawns for 1½ minutes, or until cooked through. If preferred, "butterfly" the prawns by cutting down centre back and pressing sides out flat before coating with cornflour and egg. Cooking time will then be slightly shorter. Arrange on a plate and pour on the sauce.

If liked, the prawns can be served on a bed of crisp rice vermicelli. Break the rice vermicelli into short pieces. Deep-fry for a few seconds only in hot oil until puffed and white. Remove and drain.

PRAWN OMELETTE

125 g (4 oz) peeled prawns
1 tablespoon rice wine, ginger wine or dry sherry
2 teaspoons light soy sauce
pinch of white pepper
2½ tablespoons oil
2 spring onions, trimmed and chopped
4 eggs, well beaten
1 tablespoon water
salt and pepper
1 teaspoon cornflour

Sauce: (optional)
¼ cup chicken stock
1 tablespoon oyster sauce
1 teaspoon cornflour

Cut prawns into bite-sized pieces and marinate in half the wine, with the soy sauce and pepper. Heat the oil in a wok and stir-fry the prawns until they change colour. Add the white parts of the spring onions and stir-fry briefly.

Mix eggs with water, salt and pepper and cornflour. Pour over the prawns and cook over moderate heat until golden brown underneath. Cut omelette in four and turn. Cook the other side until the egg is just set. Remove to a plate.

Heat the sauce ingredients together in another pan until boiling. Pour over omelette and sprinkle chopped spring onion greens on top.

SHRIMP WITH CASHEW NUTS AND VEGETABLES

250 g (½ lb) raw shrimp
salt
pepper
1½ tablespoons cornflour
75 g (2½ oz) celery, finely diced
60 g (2 oz) baby corn cobs, drained and cut into
   1 cm (½ inch) pieces
60 g (2 oz) cucumber, chopped (optional)
45 g (1½ oz) green pepper, chopped
75 g (2½ oz) button mushrooms or champignons,
   chopped
6 spring onions, finely chopped
60 g (2 oz) bamboo shoots, drained and chopped
oil
45 g (1½ oz) raw cashew nuts
1¾ cups chicken or fish stock
1 teaspoon salt
½ teaspoon white pepper
3 teaspoons dark soy sauce
1 tablespoon Chinese rice wine
fresh coriander leaves

Peel and devein shrimps and sprinkle with salt and pepper. Coat lightly with cornflour.

Put all vegetables in a saucepan and pour in stock, reserving 3 tablespoons. Bring to the boil and season with salt and pepper. Cook for 2 minutes, then remove from heat and drain.

Heat oil and gently deep fry cashews for 5 minutes. Heat 2 tablespoons oil and stir-fry shrimp for 2 minutes. Add vegetables and a little more oil if necessary and stir-fry for 2 minutes on high heat. Add salt, pepper, soy sauce and Chinese wine, stir, then pour in reserved stock. Thicken sauce with a little cornflour mixed with cold water and continue to cook until sauce clears.

Stir in fried cashew nuts. Spoon onto a warmed serving plate and garnish with fresh coriander leaves.

SPICY PRAWNS

8 medium raw prawns
½ fresh red chilli
1 spring onion
1 teaspoon spiced salt
2 cloves garlic
1 teaspoon cornflour
3 tablespoons oil

Soak prawns in cold water for 10 minutes. Slice chillies and spring onion thinly. Trim legs off prawns and wipe dry. Season with half the spiced salt and leave for 15 minutes. Drain and sprinkle on cornflour.

Heat oil and fry garlic for ½ minute. Add prawns and fry until pink and cooked through. Add chilli and remaining spiced salt and stir on moderate heat for ½ minute. Transfer to a serving dish and serve at once.

CRYSTAL PRAWNS

24 medium sized raw prawns
1 tablespoon ginger wine (see glossary)
1 tablespoon water
¼ teaspoon white pepper
4 spring onions
2.5 cm (1 inch) piece fresh ginger, sliced
1 carrot, sliced
oil

Peel away shells from prawns leaving heads and tails intact. With a small sharp knife cut a deep slit down the back of each prawn and scrape out the dark vein. Cut almost through the prawn. Marinate in ginger wine, water and pepper for 5 minutes.

Clean spring onions and cut into 8 cm (3 inch) pieces. Shred both ends of each piece and drop into a dish of iced water to curl. Cut decorative shapes from carrot and ginger slices using a vegetable cutter.

Heat about 3 tablespoons oil in a *wok* and stir-fry prawns until they turn pink and curl. Cook until flesh is just firm. Do not overcook. Lift onto a serving plate and decorate with spring onion curls, and sliced ginger and carrot. Serve with a bowl of dark soya sauce.

SCALLOPS WITH SHRIMP AND MUSHROOMS

12 large fresh scallops
220 g (7 oz) raw shrimp, peeled
2 teaspoons Chinese rice wine
2 teaspoons light soy sauce
6 dried Chinese mushrooms, soaked
6 canned or fresh straw mushrooms
1 cm (½ inch) piece fresh ginger, shredded
4 spring onions, shredded
1½ tablespoons oil
1 teaspoon sugar
salt
white pepper
⅔ cup light chicken or fish stock
1 heaped teaspoon cornflour
2 egg whites

Wash scallops in salted water and drain well. Cut shrimps open down the backs and scrape out dark veins. Wash well. Place scallops and shrimp in a dish and pour on wine and soy sauce. Marinate for 10 minutes.

Drain mushrooms and remove stems. Cut in halves. Lightly boil fresh straw mushrooms or drain canned mushrooms and rinse in cold water. Cut in halves.

Heat oil and fry ginger and spring onions for 1 minute. Add scallops and cook for 2 minutes, then add mushrooms and season with sugar, salt and pepper. Add shrimp and cook for another minute on moderate to low heat. Pour in stock and bring to the boil. Thicken with cornflour mixed with a little cold water. Stir in lightly beaten egg whites which will form white threads in the sauce. Do not stir again until egg sets. Transfer to a serving dish and serve at once.

CHICKEN

ONE-POT CHICKEN WITH RICE AND CHINESE SAUSAGE

375 g (¾ lb) short grain rice
3 cups light chicken stock
185 g (6 oz) chicken breast
3 dried Chinese mushrooms, soaked
1 dried Chinese sausage
2 spring onions, shredded
pinch of salt
white pepper
½ teaspoon sugar
1 tablespoon light soy sauce
1 teaspoon sesame oil
1 teaspoon cornflour
1 tablespoon water

Wash rice and put into a casserole with chicken stock. Bring to the boil, cover and reduce heat. Cook until beginning to soften and water reduced to the level of the rice. Cut chicken into 2.5 cm (1 inch) cubes and scatter over the rice. Drain and slice mushrooms, wash and slice sausage. Add to the pot with remaining ingredients. Cover and continue to cook until the rice is done and meat tender. Any liquid in the pot should be absorbed into the rice. Stir with chopsticks to distribute meat through the rice. Serve at once.

SANG CHOY POW

500 g (1 lb) chicken breast
1 tablespoon dark soy sauce
1 teaspoon sugar
2 teaspoons rice wine, ginger wine or dry sherry
2 Chinese sausages, finely chopped
4 dried Chinese mushrooms, soaked and chopped
100 g (3½ oz) canned bamboo shoots, chopped
3 spring onions, chopped
1–2 cloves garlic, chopped
2 cm (¾ inch) piece fresh ginger, chopped
2 cups oil
3–4 tablespoons sweet bean paste (*hoisin* sauce)
salt and white pepper
chilli oil (optional)
60 g (2 oz) rice vermicelli (optional)
12 medium sized lettuce leaves

Coarsely mince the chicken and season with soy sauce, sugar and wine. Leave for 10 minutes. Prepare the sausages and vegetables. Stir-fry together in 4 tablespoons of the oil for about 4 minutes. Add the chicken and continue to stir-fry until the chicken has changed colour. Add 1 tablespoon of the bean paste with salt and pepper to taste, adding a little more soy sauce and a dash of chilli oil if desired.

Heat the remaining oil in another pan and deep-fry broken rice vermicelli (if used) until crisp. Remove from the oil before it begins to colour too much. Stir the vermicelli into the meat.

To serve, pile the meat and vermicelli onto a lettuce leaf and add a little *hoisin* sauce. Roll up to enclose the filling and eat with the fingers.

BEGGAR'S CHICKEN

2 kg (4 lb) chicken
12 dried Chinese mushrooms, soaked
155 g (5 oz) Tientsin preserved vegetables
100 g (3½ oz) fat pork
3 tablespoons oil
1 tablespoon dark soy sauce
2 teaspoons Chinese rice wine
2 teaspoons sugar
pinch of white pepper
4 lotus leaves (or use spinach or cabbage)
newspaper or plain paper
1½ kg (3 lb) clay or plain flour

Wash and wipe chicken. Drain and chop mushrooms and preserved vegetables. Dice pork finely. Saute pork in oil until cooked through. Add mushrooms, vegetables and all seasonings and stir-fry for 5 minutes. Cool slightly. Stuff the mixture into the cavity of the bird and secure the opening with toothpicks or sew up carefully.

Cover chicken with lotus leaves, or other leaves. Wrap in newspaper or plain paper and encase in the prepared clay. If using flour, make into a stiff dough with water and wrap the paste around the bird after first wrapping in paper. Ensure there are no cracks which will allow the juices to escape. Place on a baking sheet in a moderately hot oven for 1¾-2 hours. The bird should be so tender that the flesh falls from the bones.

Break open casing and tear away paper and leaves before serving.

CHICKEN WINGS BRAISED IN OYSTER SAUCE

12 chicken wings
1 tablespoon dark soy sauce
oil for deep frying
8 stalks Chinese cabbage or spring greens
1 teaspoon sesame oil
pinch each of salt and white pepper
2 tablespoons sugar (or to taste)
½ cup water

Cut the chicken wings at the main joint, and cut off wing tips. Place in a dish, pour on soy sauce and rub well into the skin to colour. Leave for 10 minutes. Deep-fry until well browned.

Cut vegetables into 8 cm (3 inch) sections and drop into a saucepan of boiling salted water. Cook until tender, then lift out and drain very well. Transfer 3 tablespoons of the deep oil to a wok or pan and stir-fry vegetables for 2 minutes. Season with sesame oil, salt and pepper, and arrange on a serving dish. Keep warm.

Place the chicken wings in the pan and add the oyster sauce, sugar and water. Simmer until the wings are tender, adding more water if needed to keep the wings moist. Check seasonings, arrange the wings on the vegetables and serve.

CHICKEN WITH WALNUTS

375 g (¾ lb) chicken breast
1 egg white
1 tablespoon cornflour
1 tablespoon ginger wine (see glossary)
½ teaspoon salt
pinch of white pepper
1 teaspoon sesame oil
1 teaspoon vegetable oil
185 g (6 oz) shelled walnuts
salt
oil for deep frying
2 spring onions, chopped in 2.5 cm (1 inch) lengths
1 cm (½ inch) piece fresh ginger, sliced
1½ teaspoons Chinese rice wine
1½ teaspoons soy sauce
pinch of white pepper
½ teaspoon sesame oil
1½ tablespoons water
cornflour

Skin chicken and cut into 2.5 cm (1 inch) cubes. Put into a basin and add egg white and cornflour. Mix well. Pour on ginger wine, salt, sesame oil, and vegetable oil and stir well. Leave to marinate for 10 minutes.

Put walnuts into a saucepan, cover with water and add 1 teaspoon salt. Bring to the boil, then reduce heat and simmer for 10 minutes. Drain and dry on a kitchen towel. Heat oil to smoking point and lower in walnuts on a perforated ladle. Fry until deep golden brown. Lift out and drain well.

Reheat oil and put in the chicken pieces. Deep fry until lightly coloured, then lift out and drain. Pour off all but 2 tablespoons oil and add spring onions and ginger. Fry for one minute, then add chicken pieces and remaining seasonings. Stir-fry for 30 seconds. Add walnuts and cornflour mixed with water. Stir until the sauce thickens slightly and becomes clear. Check seasonings.

Note: Dried chillies, bamboo shoots, carrots or cashew nuts may be used in place of walnuts.

PAPER-WRAPPED CHICKEN

375 g (¾ lb) chicken
3 teaspoons sesame oil
2 teaspoons salt
1 teaspoon Chinese five-spice powder
¼ teaspoon crushed star anise
heavy-duty cellophane or greaseproof paper
oil for deep frying

Cut chicken into small dice. Mix remaining ingredients and pour over the chicken. Mix well and leave to marinate for ½ hour. Cut cellophane into 20 cm (8 inch) squares. Divide meat between the paper sheets and fold up, tucking the last end in securely.

Heat oil to smoking point and carefully lower in the packages. Deep fry for 1½-2 minutes. Lift out and drain thoroughly before serving, still in paper wrapping. Each diner unwraps his chicken just before eating.

STIR-FRIED CHICKEN AND GREEN PEPPERS

375 g (¾ lb) chicken breasts
1 egg white, beaten
5 tablespoons cornflour
1 tablespoon light soy sauce
2 teaspoons rice wine, ginger wine or dry sherry
¼ teaspoon white pepper
2 green peppers
1 fresh red chilli
2 cloves garlic
2 teaspoons salted black beans
5 tablespoons oil
¾ cup chicken stock

Skin the chicken if necessary and cut into 2.5 cm (1 inch) cubes. Combine egg white, 4 teaspoons cornflour, soy sauce, wine and pepper and pour over chicken. Marinate for 15 minutes.

Cut green peppers into narrow strips. Chop chilli, garlic and black beans. Stir-fry chicken in oil until just cooked through, remove and keep warm. Stir-fry green peppers until beginning to soften. Add the black bean mixture and cook for 1 minute. Return the chicken, add the stock mixed with remaining cornflour, and stir until the sauce thickens slightly and becomes clear. Check seasonings and serve.

LEMON CHICKEN

1½ kg (3 lb) chicken
salt and white pepper
1½ teaspoons sugar
½ tablespoon rice wine, ginger or dry sherry
2 tablespoons tapioca flour or cornflour
2 egg yolks
oil for deep frying

Sauce:
juice of 2 lemons (½ cup)
3 tablespoons sugar (or to taste)
1½ teaspoons chicken stock powder
1 cup water
1 cm (½ inch) piece fresh ginger, shredded (optional)
natural yellow food colouring (optional)
1¼ tablespoons cornflour
lemon slices

Prepare chicken, rinse and pat dry. Mix salt and pepper with sugar and wine and rub into the chicken inside and out. Leave for 15 minutes. Place in a steamer and cook for 45 minutes. Leave to cool. Make a thin batter of flour, egg yolks and a little water and paint over the chicken.

Heat oil and carefully lower in the bird. Deep-fry until the skin is golden brown and crisp. Lift out and drain well; then cut into serving pieces.

Put all the sauce ingredients into a small saucepan and bring to the boil, stirring until mixture becomes clear. Check taste and add more sugar or lemon as preferred. Pour over the chicken and garnish with lemon slices.

SLICED CHICKEN WITH HAM AND VEGETABLES

1½ kg (3 lb) chicken
2 tablespoons rice wine, ginger wine or dry sherry
4 teaspoons sugar
1 teaspoon salt
⅓ teaspoon white pepper
2 spring onions, shredded
2.5 cm (1 inch) piece fresh ginger, shredded
2 teaspoons sesame oil
125 g (¼ lb) Chinese or other cured ham
1 bunch Chinese green vegetables
cornflour

Clean and wipe the chicken and rub inside and out with a mixture of half the wine and sugar, and the salt and pepper. Place the onions and ginger in the cavity and place the chicken on a dish in a steamer. Steam over simmering water for about 25 minutes, until just cooked. Remove and rub the skin with sesame oil. Strain the liquid from the dish into a bowl.

Slice the ham thinly. Remove the chicken and cut into slices the same size as the ham. Arrange the chicken and ham alternately in rows on a dish, slightly overlapped, with the vegetable stems between the rows. Surround with the vegetable leaves. Place in the steamer and cook until the vegetables are tender and the chicken done.

Strain the liquid which has accumulated in the dish into a saucepan or wok and add the reserved steaming liquid. Stir in a little cornflour and bring to the boil. Stir until thickened, adding salt and pepper to taste. Pour over the dish and serve at once.

CRISP SKIN PEKING CHICKEN

1½ kg (3 lb) chicken
2 tablespoons rice wine, ginger wine or dry sherry
1 teaspoon salt
1 teaspoon sugar
2 teaspoons sesame oil
¼ teaspoon white pepper
¾ teaspoon Chinese five-spice powder
2 egg whites, well beaten
¾ cup cornflour
oil for deep frying

Rinse the chicken, drain and wipe dry. Rub all over with a mixture of wine, salt, sugar, sesame oil, pepper and five-spice powder. Let stand for ½ hour. Pat dry, brush with egg white and coat fairly thickly with cornflour.

Heat oil to smoking point and lower in the bird on a large perforated ladle. Splash oil over the chicken to seal the surfaces, then reduce heat and fry until golden brown. Remove the chicken and let stand for 10 minutes.

Reheat the oil. Return the chicken to cook another 5 minutes. Remove and let stand again, then return to hot oil to cook until the surface is golden brown and crisp and the chicken is cooked through. Drain and cut into serving pieces. Serve with spiced salt.

DUCK

FRIED TARO-STUFFED DUCKLING

1½ kg (3 lb) duckling
2 spring onions, shredded
1 cm (½ inch) piece fresh ginger, shredded
2 star anise
3 teaspoons rice wine, ginger wine or dry sherry
2 tablespoons dark soy sauce
1 teaspoon sugar
1 teaspoon five-spice powder
½ teaspoon black pepper
beaten egg
cornflour
oil for deep frying

Stuffing:
375 g (¾ lb) cooked taro or yam
4 dried Chinese mushrooms, soaked
2 tablespoons finely chopped fresh coriander leaves
1 teaspoon sesame oil
salt and sugar to taste
1 tablespoon softened lard
1 tablespoon cornflour
1–2 egg whites, beaten

Rinse duck and drain well. Wipe inside and out. Place spring onions, ginger and star anise in the cavity and rub skin with a mixture of wine, soy sauce, sugar, five-spice powder and pepper. Leave to absorb flavours for 15 minutes.

Put duck onto a plate in a steamer and cook over gently simmering water for about 1½ hours, until very tender. Leave to cool, then cut in halves down the centre back. Carefully pull away all bones and press the duck out flat.

Mash cooked taro and mix with mushrooms, coriander, sesame oil and sugar, working to a smooth paste. Work in lard, cornflour and egg white to bind the stuffing. Spread thickly over the inside of the duck halves and press on gently with the fingers. Brush with beaten egg and coat in cornflour.

Heat deep oil to smoking point, then lower heat slightly. Carefully lift the duck into the oil and deep-fry until dark brown and the skin is very crisp. Lift out and drain well. Cut into serving pieces and arrange on a plate. Serve with small dishes of soy, chilli and *hoisin* sauces.

Lemon Chicken (recipe page 22).

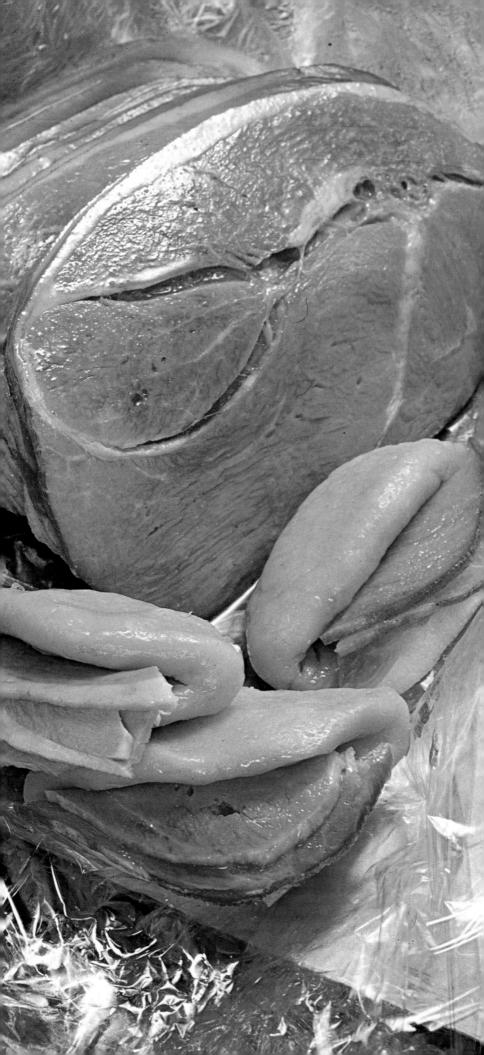

PEKING DUCK WITH PANCAKES

This simplified version of the long and involved traditional recipe gives good results.

3 kg (6 lb) fat duck
boiling water
1 cup golden syrup
1 heaped teaspoon Chinese five-spice powder
3 star anise, whole

Pancakes:
185 g (6 oz) plain flour
½ cup boiling water
sesame oil

Garnishes:
spring onion curls
sweet bean paste or *hoisin* sauce

Clean and rinse duck. Dry thoroughly. Suspend on a metal hook over a large bowl and pour boiling water into the cavity and over the skin. Dilute golden syrup with enough boiling water to make it liquid enough to pour. Pat the bird dry and rub evenly with five-spice powder. Pour on syrup, allowing some to run into the cavity. Place star anise in the cavity and close the opening with a thin metal skewer. Leave the duck to hang for about 5 hours, directing air from a fan over it to dry the skin. This process makes the skin crisp when cooked.

Brush the bird with any remaining syrup solution and place on a rack in a baking tin. Roast in a preheated moderately hot oven for 1 hour. Turn and roast for a further ¾ hour or until cooked through. Test if done by inserting a skewer into the thickest part of the thigh. If no pink liquid escapes, the bird is done. Avoid overcooking. Remove from oven to stand for at least 10 minutes before carving.

To prepare pancakes, sieve flour into a mixing bowl and pour in water. Work with a wooden spoon until dough is completely amalgamated. Add a little more water if needed. When cool enough to handle transfer to a floured board and knead briskly for 10 minutes. Cover with a damp cloth and leave to stand in a warm place for 15 minutes. Roll on a floured board into a long sausage. Cut off walnut-sized pieces and press flat. Brush one side with sesame oil and stick two pieces together, oiled sides meeting. Roll out the two pancakes together until paper thin.

Heat a heavy frying pan or hot plate and cook pressed-together pancakes on moderate heat until brown flecks appear. Turn and cook other side, then peel apart. Do not cook the inside surfaces. Cook all pancakes in this way and keep wrapped in a cloth until ready to serve.

To prepare spring onion curls, cut off the lower white section and shred with a sharp knife at each end, discarding green tops. Drop into a bowl of very iced water to make them curl.

To serve Peking Duck, first slice off the skin, then the meat. Arrange on a serving plate. Serve pancakes and spring onions on another plate with sauce in small dishes for dipping. Dip a slice each of meat and skin into the sauce and place with a piece of spring onion on a pancake. Roll up to eat.

25

Honey Baked Ham (recipe page 28).

DUCK IN LEMON SOUP

1 kg (2 lb) duck pieces
6 cups water
2 lemons
2 dried tangerine peels (optional)
1 teaspoon salt
pinch of white pepper
fresh coriander sprigs

Clean duck and wipe dry. Put into a deep casserole and add water, halved lemons and tangerine peel. Add salt and white pepper. Cover and cook over low heat for about 4 hours until duck is very tender. Adjust seasonings to taste and garnish with fresh coriander before serving.

DUCK WITH CHINESE SPICES

1½ kg (3 lb) duckling
1 tablespoon spiced salt
¼ teaspoon ground Sichuan peppercorns
2 teaspoons Chinese rice wine
3 teaspoons dark soy sauce
oil for deep frying
1 tablespoon dark soy sauce

Clean and wipe duck inside and out. Combine all seasonings and rub well into the duck. Leave for 2 hours to absorb the flavours. Place on a plate over a steamer and cook on moderate heat for 2 hours. Remove from heat and rub with 1 tablespoon dark soy sauce.

   Heat enough oil to cover the duck in a deep pan. Lower in the duck and deep fry until very dark brown and crisp. Serve with spiced salt.

PORK

SWEET AND SOUR PORK

375 g (¾ lb) pork belly
2 egg whites
45 g (1½ oz) plain flour
30 g (1 oz) cornflour
½ teaspoon salt
1 teaspoon baking powder
1 tablespoon Chinese rice wine
3 teaspoons light soy sauce
pinch of salt
pinch of white pepper
1 cm (½ inch) piece fresh ginger, shredded
oil for deep frying

Sauce:
1 cm (½ inch) piece fresh ginger, shredded
1 medium carrot
¼ red pepper
¼ green pepper
⅓ stick celery
⅓ cucumber, peeled and seeded
1 medium onion
3 tablespoons oil
125 g (4 oz) sugar
⅓ cup white vinegar
¾ cup water or chicken stock
1 tablespoon cornflour
natural red food colouring (optional)
salt and white pepper

Cut pork belly into 2.5 cm (1 inch) cubes. Mix wine with soy sauce, salt, white pepper and ginger and pour over the meat. Rub in well and leave to stand for 10 minutes.

Beat egg whites with plain flour, cornflour, salt and baking powder, adding just enough water to make a smooth, fairly thick batter.

Heat oil to smoking point and lower heat slightly. Coat pork pieces with the batter and put into the oil to cook for 4 minutes. Remove and drain. Turn off heat and prepare sauce.

Cut vegetables into small dice and saute in oil until softened. Add sugar and cook until it begins to caramelize; then add vinegar and bring to the boil. Mix chicken stock or water with cornflour, pour into the pan and bring to the boil. Simmer, stirring, until the sauce thickens and clears. Add a few drops of red food colouring, if liked, and season to taste with salt and pepper.

Reheat oil and return pork pieces to fry for a further minute. Place on a serving dish and pour on the piping-hot sauce.

BARBECUED SPARE RIBS

1¼ kg (2½ lb) pork spare ribs
3 tablespoons dark soy sauce
1 tablespoon sweet bean paste
2 tablespoons sugar
3 cloves garlic
1 tablespoon Chinese rice wine
¼ teaspoon Chinese five-spice powder

Separate ribs and trim each neatly at the ends. Mix remaining ingredients together and pour over the ribs. Allow to marinate for 2 hours.

Place ribs on a rack and cook under a moderate grill until cooked through and crispy on the surface, or cook over a charcoal barbecue. Brush with the marinating liquid during cooking to keep meat moist.

HONEY BAKED HAM

750 g (1½ lb) middle section of uncooked ham
3 tablespoons honey
45 g (1½ oz) sugar
3 tablespoons oil
1 large sheet cellophane paper
2 lotus leaves (optional)
aluminium foil

Steam ham for 30 minutes, then remove skin, fat and bone and cut into thin slices. Mix honey, sugar and oil. Arrange ham slices on the cellophane paper in a block and pour on the honey mixture. Wrap cellophane around the ham, then wrap in lotus leaves or foil.

Place ham on a baking tray and bake in a moderate oven for 2 hours. Leave to cool for 15 minutes before removing the wrappers.

STEWED PORK WITH TARO

1 kg (2 lb) pork belly with rind
½ cup dark soy sauce
500 g (1 lb) peeled taro or yam
5 cloves garlic
4 cubes fermented beancurd "cheese"
1½ tablespoons rice wine, ginger wine or dry sherry
1 teaspoon sugar
¾ teaspoon white pepper
3 tablespoons oil
250 g (½ lb) Chinese cabbage

Place the pork in a dish, pour on the soy sauce and marinate for 20 minutes. Cut the taro into cubes. Finely chop the garlic and mix with mashed beancurd, wine, sugar and pepper. Cut the pork into slices and fry in the oil until lightly coloured.

Chop the cabbage and spread in the bottom of a casserole. Layer the pork and taro on top. Mix the beancurd seasoning with 1 cup of water, pour over the dish, adding enough extra water to cover. Set in a steamer to cook for about 1½ hours, until the meat is very tender.

SHREDDED PORK WITH VERMICELLI IN SESAME BUNS

125 g (¼ lb) lean pork
90 g (3 oz) transparent vermicelli
3 tablespoons oil
1 cm (½ inch) piece fresh ginger, finely shredded
3 spring onions, finely shredded
3 teaspoons hot bean paste
1 teaspoon salt
2 tablespoons dark soy sauce
1 teaspoon sugar
1 cup beef stock
2 teaspoons cornflour
2 teaspoons sesame oil

Slice pork thinly, then cut into thin shreds. Soak vermicelli in warm water to soften. Drain and cut into 2.5 cm (1 inch) pieces. Heat oil and fry pork until well coloured. Add ginger and spring onions and fry for 2 minutes, then add bean paste and stir on moderate heat for 1 minute. Add vermicelli and salt, soy sauce, sugar and stock. Bring to the boil and simmer until pork and vermicelli are tender and liquid almost absorbed.

Mix cornflour with a very little cold water and stir into the meat. Leave to thicken slightly, then sprinkle on sesame oil. Serve with crispy sesame buns. Cut the buns in halves and stuff with the pork and vermicelli mixture.

Sesame Buns:
1 cup plain flour
¾ cup vegetable oil
750 g (1½ lb) plain flour
1½ cups boiling water
cold water
1½ teaspoons salt
30 g (1 oz) white sesame seeds

Pour 1 cup plain flour and vegetable oil into a pan and fry on moderate heat, stirring, until the flour is coloured a rich golden brown and is very fragrant. Leave the flour oil to cool.

Sieve remaining 750 g (1½ lb) flour into a mixing bowl and add boiling water. Work with chopsticks until incorporated, then add cold water and salt to make a smooth, fairly stiff dough. Knead for 10 minutes on a lightly floured board. Cover with a damp cloth and leave for 15 minutes, then knead for a further 5 minutes. Roll out to about 2 mm (1/16 inch) thick. Spread the flour oil thickly over the dough and roll up into a long tube. Cut into 2.5 cm (1 inch) lengths.

Roll each piece out across the folds, fold two ends in and turn the dough to one side. Roll out again, working away from the body. Continue rolling, folding and rolling for about five times. Press sesame seeds onto each piece and roll out into a 13 cm (5 inch) long cake, about 4 cm (1½ inches) wide. Place on a floured baking sheet and bake in a preheated hot oven for 7 minutes, turn and cook the other side for about 3 minutes. Cool slightly before cutting in halves.

BEEF

BEEF IN OYSTER SAUCE

500 g (1 lb) tender beef steak
2 teaspoons sugar
1 tablespoon cornflour
2 tablespoons dark soy sauce
1 tablespoon rice wine, ginger wine or dry sherry
1½ teaspoons sesame oil
5 tablespoons oil
12 dried Chinese mushrooms, soaked
⅓ green pepper
⅓ red pepper
1 medium onion
3 tablespoons oyster sauce
sugar to taste
cornflour

Slice the beef very thinly and cut into 5 cm (2 inch) strips. Mix sugar, cornflour, soy sauce, wine and sesame oil in a dish. Add 2 tablespoons oil and mix well. Pour over the steak and leave for 15 minutes.

Drain mushrooms and reserve soaking liquid. Squeeze the mushrooms, and trim off the stems. Cut the peppers and onion into narrow strips. Stir-fry mushrooms, peppers and onion in 3 tablespoons oil until softened, then remove. Stir-fry the steaks over high heat until very lightly cooked, and remove. Add the mushroom water, oyster sauce and sugar to the pan. Bring to the boil, add a little cornflour mixed with cold water, and stir until thickened. Return the meat and vegetables to the sauce and stir. Serve at once.

SICHUAN BEEF STEW

1 kg (2 lb) stewing beef, preferably shin or flank
3 whole star anise
1 large onion, sliced
2.5 cm (1 inch) piece fresh ginger, sliced
1 dried tangerine peel or 1 lemon rind
2 tablespoons oil
6 cloves garlic
2 teaspoons black peppercorns, crushed
2 teaspoons Chinese brown peppercorns
¾ cup dark soy sauce
¼ cup Chinese rice wine
3 tablespoons sweet bean paste or *hoisin* sauce

Cut meat into 5 cm (2 inch) cubes. Place in a deep pot and cover with water. Add star anise, onion, ginger and tangerine peel or lemon rind. Cover and bring to the boil, then reduce heat and simmer for at least 2 hours.

Heat oil in a small saucepan and add chopped garlic and peppercorns. Fry for 1 minute, then add soy sauce, wine and bean paste or *hoisin* sauce. Bring to the boil and remove from the heat. Skim off any froth and pour the sauce into the meat. Cover and cook for a further 1 hour. Remove star anise and peel before serving.

SHREDDED BEEF WITH BAMBOO SHOOTS

250 g (½ lb) topside beef
125 g (¼ lb) canned bamboo shoots
4 spring onions
2.5 cm (1 inch) piece fresh ginger, sliced
1 clove garlic (optional)
1 tablespoon dark soy sauce
3 teaspoons oil
2 teaspoons Chinese rice wine
2 teaspoons cornflour
½ teaspoon salt
pinch of white pepper
1 teaspoon sugar
3 tablespoons oil

Slice meat thinly across the grain, then into strips about 4 cm by 0.5 cm (1½ inches by ¼ inch). Drain and shred bamboo shoots. Cut spring onions into 2.5 cm (1 inch) pieces and shred ginger slices. Crush garlic (if used). Mix ingredients from soy sauce to white pepper and pour over meat. Leave to marinate for 15 minutes.

Heat oil in a *wok* and stir-fry beef until well coloured. Add bamboo shoots, spring onion, ginger and garlic and pour on any remaining marinade. Add a little water and cook for another minute. Add sugar and if necessary thicken sauce with a little cornflour mixed with cold water. Stir on moderate to high heat until sauce thickens and clears.

VEGETABLES

SAUTE OF GREEN VEGETABLES WITH CRABMEAT DRESSING

500 g (1 lb) Chinese cabbage or Chinese long leaf
  lettuce
4 cups water
2 tablespoons oil
½ teaspoon salt
90 g (3 oz) cooked or canned crabmeat
2 teaspoons cornflour
⅓ cup water
2 egg whites
salt
white pepper
1 teaspoon light soy sauce
½ teaspoon sesame oil
3 teaspoons crab roe, crumbled (optional)

Wash cabbage or lettuce and shake out water. Break leaves from stem, discarding centre core. Bring water to boil with 1 tablespoon oil and when bubbling put in cabbage or lettuce. Reduce heat slightly and cook cabbage for 30-40 seconds, lettuce for a maximum of 20 seconds. Lift out and drain well. Arrange vegetables on a serving dish and splash with remaining oil.

Flake crabmeat and put into a small saucepan with cornflour mixed with water. Bring to the boil and stir until slightly thickened. When sauce is just bubbling slowly, pour in beaten egg white so it forms white threads in the sauce. Do not stir until the egg sets. Season with salt, white pepper and soy sauce. Pour dressing over the vegetable and sprinkle on sesame oil and crab roe.

TWO-COLOUR MUSHROOMS

10 dried Chinese mushrooms, soaked
1 teaspoon Chinese rice wine
1½ tablespoons dark soy sauce
1 teaspoon sugar
2 tablespoons chicken stock
1 tablespoon oil
15 canned white straw mushrooms or champignons
salt
¼ cup chicken stock
¼ cup fresh milk
1½ teaspoons cornflour

Remove stems from dried mushrooms and place in a dish with rice wine, soy sauce, sugar, chicken stock and oil. Cover and steam on high heat for 30 minutes.

Drain straw mushrooms or champignons. Boil with a little salt and chicken for 3 minutes. Drain well. Arrange black dried mushrooms on one side of a serving dish and white mushrooms on the other side.

Pour juices from black mushrooms into a small saucepan and add chicken stock and milk. Thicken with cornflour mixed with a little cold water. Bring to the boil and cook until thick. Add salt to taste and pour over the vegetables. Serve at once.

FRIED BEANCURD

8 squares soft beancurd
vegetable or peanut oil
2 tablespoons light soy sauce
1 tablespoon spiced salt powder

Choose well-drained, fairly firm pieces of beancurd. Wrap beancurd in a towel, put in dish, and place flat weight on top. Leave to drain and firm for at least 8 hours.

Wipe beancurd and place several pieces on a large perforated ladle. Heat oil to smoking point, then lower heat slightly. Carefully lower the ladle into the oil and leave until beancurd has cooked to a light golden colour. Lift out and drain thoroughly, then transfer beancurd to a serving dish. Cook remaining beancurd pieces and add to the plate.

Sprinkle with soy sauce and serve with a dip of spiced salt.

STIR-FRIED VEGETABLE ASSORTMENT

8 dried Chinese mushrooms
250 g (½ lb) snow peas *(mange-tout)*
250 g (½ lb) canned bamboo shoots
1 small carrot
90 g (3 oz) frozen green peas
2 tablespoons oil
½ teaspoon salt
½ teaspoon sugar
1½ teaspoons dark soy sauce
2 teaspoons Chinese rice wine
¼ cup chicken stock
½ teaspoon cornflour
½ teaspoon sesame oil

Soak mushrooms in cold water for ½ hour. Wash snow peas and remove strings. Drain bamboo shoots and slice thinly. Scrape and slice carrot and cut into decorative shapes with a vegetable cutter. Thaw peas. Drop carrots into a small saucepan of boiling water to simmer for 2 minutes. Drain well. Drain mushrooms and slice thinly.

Heat oil in a *wok* and fry bamboo shoots with carrots for 1½ minutes. Season with salt, sugar, soy sauce and Chinese wine and add mushrooms and snow peas. Stir-fry for another 1½ minutes, then put in peas and add chicken stock. Bring to a rapid boil and continue to stir vegetables until the liquid is reduced.

Thicken sauce with cornflour mixed with cold water and sprinkle on sesame oil before serving.

COMBINATION OMELETTE

4 eggs
60 g (2 oz) Chinese roast pork
60 g (2 oz) canned bamboo shoots
3 dried Chinese mushrooms, soaked
1 small carrot
1 cm (½ inch) piece fresh ginger
8 chive or spring onion shoots
1 spring onion
pinch of salt
white pepper
1 teaspoon sesame oil
1 teaspoon cornflour
2 tablespoons water
3 tablespoons oil
fresh coriander leaves or fresh red chilli

Beat eggs lightly and set aside. Cut roast pork and bamboo shoots into thin shreds. Drain mushrooms and cut into thin shreds. Scrape carrot and cut into matchstick pieces. Shred ginger, chive or spring onion shoots and cut spring onion into 2.5 cm (1 inch) lengths.

Season eggs with salt and pepper. Add sesame oil, cornflour mixed with water and set aside. Heat oil and fry meat and vegetables until slightly softened. Pour in egg and stir vegetables evenly through the egg. Cook on low heat until egg is set underneath. Cut in halves or quarters and turn. Cook other side, then slide onto a serving plate. Garnish with sprigs of fresh coriander or shreds of red chilli.

BRAISED BEANCURD WITH CHINESE MUSHROOMS

4 squares soft beancurd
oil for deep frying
6 dried Chinese mushrooms, soaked
4 spring onions
½ cup chicken stock
1 tablespoon dark soy sauce
1 tablespoon oyster sauce
1 teaspoon sugar
1 teaspoon cornflour
1 teaspoon sesame oil

Choose firm pieces of beancurd. Cut each square of beancurd into quarters and place on a large perforated ladle. Heat oil to smoking point and lower in the beancurd to deep fry to a dark brown. Remove and drain well.

Drain mushrooms and remove stems. Cut spring onions into 2.5 cm (1 inch) pieces. Heat about 3 tablespoons oil in a *wok* and fry mushrooms and spring onions for 3 minutes. Add chicken stock, dark soy sauce, oyster sauce and sugar and bring to the boil. Add beancurd and cover. Braise until the mushrooms are completely tender and sauce well reduced.

Thicken with cornflour mixed with a little cold water and stir carefully until the sauce clears. Sprinkle on sesame oil and serve hot.

MA PO BEANCURD

½ cup oil
6 squares soft beancurd
90 g (3 oz) minced beef
90 g (3 oz) minced pork
8 cloves garlic, finely chopped
4 spring onions, finely chopped
1½ tablespoons hot bean paste
¼ teaspoon white pepper, or
    1½ teaspoons chilli oil
3 tablespoons dark soya sauce
½ cup beef stock
2 teaspoons cornflour
1½ teaspoons sesame oil

Choose well-drained firm pieces of beancurd. Heat oil in a frying pan. Drain beancurd and hold in the palm of the hand. Carefully cut into cubes, then transfer to a slice and lower into the pan. Fry the beancurd without stirring to avoid breaking the cubes. Cook to a light golden brown. Lift out and set aside.

Add minced beef and pork to the pan and fry to a light brown before adding garlic, onion, bean paste, pepper or chilli oil and soy sauce. Cook for 3 minutes, then add beef stock mixed with cornflour.

Bring to the boil, reduce heat and simmer until sauce is thickened and meat is well seasoned. Return beancurd and cook for 2 minutes. Transfer to a serving dish and splash with sesame oil.

EGGPLANT SICHUAN STYLE

375 g (¾ lb) eggplants
4 tablespoons oil
2 teaspoons sesame oil
6 spring onions
8 cloves garlic
1 cm (½ inch) piece fresh ginger
2 tablespoons *hoisin* sauce
1½ teaspoons sugar
2 tablespoons dark soy sauce
1½ teaspoons Chinese brown vinegar
⅓ cup chicken or beef stock
2 teaspoons cornflour
2 teaspoons sesame oil

Wipe eggplants, remove stalks but do not peel. Cut into 2.5 cm (1 inch) thick slices. Heat oil, add sesame oil and fry both sides of sliced eggplant for 1 minute. Turn heat down and cook until soft, then remove from pan and drain on absorbent paper.

Chop spring onions, garlic and ginger finely. Add to the pan with a little more oil if needed and fry for 1 minute. Add remaining ingredients except cornflour and sesame oil and bring to the boil. Simmer for 3 minutes, then return eggplant and cook for 10 minutes on moderate to low heat. Thicken sauce with cornflour mixed with a little cold water and cook until clear. Sprinkle on sesame oil.

Thinly sliced red chilli can be added at the same time as the spring onions to make this dish more piquant.

SICHUAN PICKLE

1 carrot
250 g (½ lb) Chinese cabbage
2 medium cucumbers
1 giant white radish
4 fresh red chillies
2.5 cm (1 inch) piece fresh ginger
3 tablespoons Chinese rice wine
5 cups boiling water
1 tablespoon lightly crushed black peppercorns
45 g (1½ oz) salt
15 g (½ oz) sugar

Scrape and slice carrot. Wash and chop cabbage coarsely. Wipe and slice cucumbers (peel if preferred). Peel and slice radish. Slice red chillies and ginger. Put all ingredients into several large jars. Add remaining ingredients, seal jars and shake well. Leave for about 4 days in a dark, dry cupboard.

To use, remove pickles from the liquid and transfer to smaller jars. Store tightly sealed until needed. The pickling liquid may be used for a second pickling.

HOTPOT OF VEGETABLES AND BEANCURD

This hotpot is made in the kitchen in an earthenware cooking pot and carried to the table steaming hot.

8 squares soft beancurd
1 medium carrot
12 dried Chinese mushrooms, soaked
4 spring onions
60 g (2 oz) canned bamboo shoots
30 g (1 oz) 'cloud ear' fungus, soaked
100 g (3½ oz) chicken livers or pigs liver
8 cups water or chicken stock
soy sauce to taste
Chinese brown vinegar to taste

Slice or dice beancurd and set aside. Scrape carrot and slice thinly. Drain mushrooms and cut each in half. Chop spring onions. Thinly slice bamboo shoots. Drain 'cloud ear' fungus. Clean and slice chicken livers or pigs liver.

Bring stock to boil in an earthenware pot and drop in the carrot, mushrooms, spring onions, bamboo shoots, fungus and pigs liver (if used). Boil for 10 minutes, then add beancurd and chicken livers. Simmer gently for a further 10 minutes. Season to taste with soy sauce and/or Chinese brown vinegar.

Shredded Beef with Bamboo Shoots, and Combination Omelette (recipes pages 31 and 34).

SOUP

WONTON SOUP

Wontons:
1 packet *wonton* wrappers
155 g (5 oz) minced pork
2 spring onions, chopped
2 tablespoons chopped fresh coriander leaves
1 cm (½ inch) piece fresh ginger
1 cloved garlic (optional)
2 teaspoons cornflour
2 teaspoons dark soy sauce
½ teaspoon sugar
½ teaspoon salt
pinch of white pepper
3 teaspoons peanut oil

Soup:
375 g (¾ lb) chicken pieces
8 dried Chinese mushrooms, soaked
12 Chinese green vegetables or spinach leaves
2 spring onions, shredded
salt and light soy sauce

Separate the *wonton* wrappers and cover with a cloth until needed. Place the minced pork in a food processor. Add the remaining *wonton* ingredients and process to a smooth paste.

To make the *wontons*, place a spoonful of the filling in the centre of a wrapper, fold diagonally in halves, damp the edges with cold water and press them together. Pinch the two outer edges together to form the *wonton* into a ring, and fold the central point outwards to complete the *wonton*. Use all of the filling.

Bring a large pot of lightly salted water to the boil. Add the *wontons* and cook until they float to the surface. Drain and cover with cold water until needed.

Chop the chicken pieces and put into a saucepan with 6 cups water. Remove mushroom stems, add mushrooms to the saucepan and bring to the boil. Partially cover and simmer for 40 minutes. Strain into another pan. Retrieve the mushrooms and cut into quarters, add to the soup with the green vegetables, *wontons*, spring onions and seasoning to taste. Simmer for 5 minutes before serving.

Hotpot of Vegetables and Beancurd (recipe page 36).

HAM AND MELON SOUP

250 g (½ lb) winter melon
125 g (¼ lb) Chinese or cured ham
2 chicken livers (optional)
6 dried Chinese mushrooms, soaked
7 cups chicken stock
2 cm (¾ inch) piece fresh ginger, sliced
2 teaspoons salt
2 teaspoons rice wine, ginger wine or dry sherry
light soy sauce
white pepper

Peel the melon and cut into 2.5 cm (1 inch) cubes. Slice ham thickly. Slice chicken livers. Place melon, ham, livers and quartered mushrooms (stems removed) into a saucepan and add the stock, ginger, salt and wine. Bring to the boil and simmer until the melon is tender. Remove the ham, cut into thin slices and return to the soup. Add soy sauce to taste. Sprinkle on white pepper.

SHARKS FIN SOUP

185 g (6 oz) dried sharks fin
5 cups water
125 g (¼ lb) chicken breast
6 dried Chinese mushrooms, soaked
60 g (2 oz) smoked ham
6 cups chicken stock
2 teaspoons dark soy sauce
salt
white pepper
3 teaspoons cornflour
Chinese brown vinegar or mustard

Soak sharks fin overnight in cold water. Rinse in several lots of cold water and pick out any debris with tweezers. Cover with water and bring to the boil. Cook on low heat for 1 hour.

Slice and shred chicken finely. Drain mushrooms and shred. Shred ham. Bring chicken stock to the boil and add chicken, mushrooms and ham. Strain sharks fin and add to the soup with soy sauce. Bring to the boil and simmer until the meat and sharks fin are tender.

Season with salt and white pepper and thicken with cornflour mixed with a little cold water. Stir until the soup thickens and clears. Serve with bowls of Chinese brown vinegar or hot mustard.

FISH SOUP WITH CELERY

375 g (¾ lb) white fish fillets
4 sticks celery
1 teaspoon salt
pinch of white pepper
1 teaspoon Chinese rice wine
½ teaspoon sugar
1 tablespoon light soy sauce
2 tablespoons cornflour
1 tablespoon dried shrimps, soaked for 3 hours
2 cm (¾ inch) piece fresh ginger, sliced
5 cups boiling water
1 fish head (optional)

Cut fillets into thin slices. Quarter-celery. Mix salt, pepper, wine, sugar and soy sauce together and rub into sliced fish. Leave for 10 minutes. Put cornflour into a plastic bag and drop in fish slices. Shake bag to coat fish thickly with cornflour.

Put dried shrimps and ginger into a large saucepan with celery, boiling water and the fish head (if used). Bring to boil and simmer for 2 minutes. Drop in fish slices and simmer for 4 minutes. Discard head before serving, if preferred. Check seasoning and serve hot.

BIRDS NEST SOUP WITH QUAIL EGGS

125 g (¼ lb) prepared birds nests
6 cups chicken stock
1-2 teaspoons light soy sauce
1 teaspoon salt
¼ teaspoon white pepper
185 g (6 oz) spinach, watercress or other green
    vegetables
1 teaspoon cornflour
2 egg whites
12 poached or boiled quail eggs (see below)

Soak birds nests for 4-5 hours in cold water. Pick out debris with tweezers, rinse well and drain. Pour into a saucepan, cover with water and bring to the boil. Cook for 2 minutes, then drain. Rinse with cold water.

Return birds nests to the saucepan and pour on chicken stock. Add seasonings. Bring to the boil, then reduce heat and simmer for 5 minutes.
Add vegetables and boil until softened.

Beat egg whites and slowly pour into the soup. They will form into white threads. Do not stir until the egg sets. Add poached or boiled eggs and heat through before serving.

Note: To poach quail eggs wipe 12 small soy sauce dishes out with an oiled paper and break an egg into each. Place in a steamer and cook until set, about 2½ minutes. To boil put into a saucepan of cold water and bring to the boil. Cook for 5 minutes, then drain and cover with cold water.

SOUR AND HOT SICHUAN SOUP

125 g (¼ lb) chicken meat
60 g (2 oz) liver
3 cloves garlic, crushed
2 teaspoons rice wine, ginger wine or dry sherry
4 spring onions, shredded
6 dried Chinese mushrooms, soaked
7 cups chicken stock
1½ tablespoons dark soy sauce
½–1 tablespoon chilli oil
2 tablespoons Chinese brown vinegar
4 eggs, beaten
185 g (6 oz) soft beancurd
chopped fresh coriander leaves
salt and white pepper

Cut the chicken into thin slices, then into shreds. Cut the liver into similar pieces. Splash on wine and sprinkle garlic on top. Set aside.

Separate the white and green parts of the onions. Drain the mushrooms, remove the stems and cut caps into shreds. Bring the stock to the boil. Add the soy sauce and chilli oil and simmer for 1 minute.

Add the chicken and liver, onion whites and mushrooms and simmer for 5 minutes. Add the brown vinegar, then slowly pour in the beaten eggs to set in threads in the soup. Add the beancurd, coriander leaves, salt and white pepper. Check seasonings, adding more soy sauce, chilli and vinegar to taste. It should be quite tart and hot.

CLEAR MUSHROOM SOUP

18 large dried Chinese mushrooms, soaked in 4 cups
    water
1 tablespoon light soy sauce
salt and white pepper
1 tablespoon rice wine, ginger wine or dry sherry
125 g (4 oz) chicken giblets
4 spring onions
2.5 cm (1 inch) piece fresh ginger, sliced
4 baby Chinese white cabbages, or 8–12 leaves of
    Chinese green vegetables

Put the mushrooms and their liquid into a saucepan, add soy sauce, salt, pepper and wine, and bring to the boil. Simmer for 1 hour, then strain the liquid into another saucepan. Add chicken giblets, 1 spring onion and half the sliced ginger. Add 4 cups cold water and bring to the boil. Simmer for 15 minutes, then strain.

Chop the remaining spring onions, reserving the green sections for another recipe. Add the onions, remaining ginger and cabbage leaves to the stock. Remove mushroom stems, add mushrooms to the soup and bring to the boil. Simmer for 10 minutes. Add extra soy sauce, salt and pepper to taste.

CHICKEN AND SWEET CORN SOUP

375 g (¾ lb) chicken breast
375 g (¾ lb) canned cream-style sweet corn
2 teaspoons salt
1 tablespoon light soy sauce
¼ teaspoon white pepper
2 egg whites
3 spring onions
1 clove garlic (optional)
4 cups chicken stock
cornflour
chopped fresh coriander leaves

Remove skin from chicken breast and cut into very small dice. Pour sweet corn into a saucepan and season with salt, soy sauce and white pepper. Gently heat through. Lightly beat egg whites. Chop onions and garlic very finely.

Bring chicken stock to boil in a large saucepan and add onion, garlic and chicken pieces. Boil for 3 minutes, then pour in beaten egg white. Stir gently so egg forms white strings in the soup. Add warmed cream-style sweet corn and stir thoroughly. Thicken soup if necessary with cornflour mixed with a little cold water. Check seasonings. Garnish with chopped fresh coriander and serve with extra soy sauce.

NOODLES

FRIED EGG NOODLES WITH BEEF AND GREEN VEGETABLES

125 g (¼ lb) frying beef steak
1 tablespoon dark soy sauce
2 teaspoons rice wine, ginger wine or dry sherry
2 teaspoons cornflour
2 teaspoons sesame oil
1 teaspoon sugar
250 g (½ lb) dried fine egg noodles
125 g (¼ lb) mixed vegetables, such as snow peas,
   sliced celery, sliced green beans, broccoli flowerets,
   Chinese green vegetables
½ cup oil
3 spring onions
1 cm (½ inch) piece fresh ginger
1 tablespoon light soy sauce
salt, pepper and sugar to taste
1 cup beef or chicken stock
2 teaspoons cornflour

Slice beef thinly, then cut into strips and marinate in
a mixture of soy sauce, wine, cornflour, sesame oil and
sugar. Leave for 15 minutes. Drop noodles into boiling
water to soften and untangle. Drain well and spread on
a tray to partially dry. Blanch vegetables in boiling
water until softened, cooking the firmer ones first.

Heat oil in a wok and stir-fry the noodles over high
heat until golden and the edges are well crisped. Transfer to a serving plate. Stir-fry the meat with onions and
ginger until the meat changes colour. Add the vegetables and stir-fry until well coated with the oil. Add
any remaining marinade and the soy sauce, with salt,
pepper and sugar to taste. Add the stock mixed with
cornflour and stir over high heat until the sauce
thickens and clears. Pour over the noodles and serve.

COLD E FU NOODLES

375 g (¾ lb) thin egg noodles
2 tablespoons vegetable oil
1 tablespoon sesame oil
125 g (¼ lb) beanshoots
125 g (¼ lb) celery
125 g (¼ lb) cooked chicken
3 tablespoons sesame paste
2 tablespoons dark soy sauce
2 tablespoons lemon juice or
    1 tablespoon white vinegar
1 fresh red chilli
4 shallots
1 cm (½ inch) piece fresh ginger
1 tablespoon sesame oil
sugar to taste
2-3 teaspoons toasted white sesame seeds

Cook noodles in boiling salted water until just tender. Drain and rinse in cold water. Drain again and pour into a serving dish. Splash on vegetable and sesame oil.

Steep beanshoots in boiling water for 2 minutes to soften. Drain. Shred celery and steep in boiling water for 4 minutes, or simmer gently, until softened but still crisp. Shred chicken. Pile beanshoots, celery and chicken onto noodles.

Mix sesame paste with soy sauce, lemon juice or vinegar and enough water to make a thin sauce. Shred chilli, shallots and ginger and add to the sauce with sesame oil and sugar to taste. Mix well and pour over the noodles. Scatter sesame seeds on top. Serve cold.

RICE RIBBON NOODLES WITH BEEF AND BROCCOLI

500 g (1 lb) rice flour noodles
250 g (½ lb) frying steak
3 teaspoons Chinese rice wine
1 teaspoon sugar
2 tablespoons dark soy sauce
2 tablespoons sweet bean paste or *hoisin* sauce
6 tablespoons oil
8 broccoli spears
4 spring onions, shredded
¾ cup beef stock
cornflour
1½ teaspoons sesame oil

Drop noodles into a pot of boiling water. Remove from heat and leave to soften for 10 minutes. Drain well and allow to dry.

Slice beef thinly across the grain, then into small pieces. Marinate in a mixture of wine, sugar, soy sauce and bean paste for 10 minutes. Heat 2 tablespoons oil and fry meat for 3 minutes. Keep warm.

Cook broccoli in salted water until tender but still crisp. Heat 4 tablespoons oil and fry broccoli with spring onion for 1 minute. Remove and add noodles, frying until slightly crisp. Remove to a serving plate. Return meat and vegetables to the pan and pour on stock. Bring to the boil, then thicken with a little cornflour mixed with cold water. Spoon over noodles and sprinkle with sesame oil.

CRISPY RICE VERMICELLI WITH CHICKEN AND VEGETABLES

185 g (6 oz) rice vermicelli
90 g (3 oz) chicken breast
30 g (1 oz) chicken livers
6 dried Chinese mushrooms, soaked
60 g (2 oz) canned bamboo shoots
90 g (3 oz) *bok choy* cabbage
2 teaspoons Chinese rice wine
1 tablespoon light soy sauce
white pepper
2 teaspoons cornflour
3 tablespoons oil
¾ cup chicken stock
1 teaspoon sesame oil
salt
white pepper
2 spring onions, shredded
oil for deep frying

Break vermicelli into 5 cm (2 inch) pieces. Slice chicken thinly and chop livers. Drain and slice mushrooms and bamboo shoots and cut *bok choy* into 5 cm (2 inch) pieces. Heat a saucepan of water until boiling and put in *bok choy*. Cook until tender, then drain.

Marinate chicken in a mixture of rice wine, soy sauce, white pepper and cornflour for 5 minutes. Heat oil and fry chicken until lightly coloured. Add livers and cook until no pink shows, then add mushroms and bamboo shoots, *bok choy* and chicken stock. Boil for 1 minute, then season with sesame oil, salt and pepper. Thicken sauce slightly with a little cornflour mixed with cold water if necessary. Add spring onions.

Heat 5 cm (2 inches) oil in a deep pan and when very hot put in noodles. They will immediately expand and become very crisp. Cook for about 30 seconds. Lift out and drain. Place on a serving plate and pour on the chicken and vegetables.

RICE

FRIED CANTONESE RICE

2½ cups short-grain white rice
3 cups water
620 g (2 oz) raw peeled shrimp
2 teaspoons rice wine, ginger wine or dry sherry
60 g (2 oz) Chinese roast pork
60 g (2 oz) frozen peas
4 dried Chinese mushrooms, soaked
1 medium onion
4 spring onions
4 tablespoons oil
1 egg, beaten
2 teaspoons sesame oil (optional)
2 tablespoons light soy sauce
salt and white pepper
finely chopped fresh coriander leaves

Place the rice and water in a heavy saucepan, cover tightly and bring to the boil. Reduce heat and cook very slowly for about 18 minutes. The rice should be plump and dry, with each grain separate.

Sprinkle wine over the shrimp and set aside.

Dice or shred pork. Drain mushrooms. Cook peas with mushrooms in lightly salted water until just tender; drain. Remove mushroom stems and shred the caps. Peel the onion and slice from top to base to give narrow, curved slices. Trim the spring onions; chop the whites and a portion of the green tops and reserve the remaining tops for another recipe.

Heat 1 tablespoon oil in a wok. Add the beaten egg and cook in a thin omelette until just firm. Turn and cook the other side, then break up with a spatula and remove. Add the remaining oil (including sesame oil, if used) and stir-fry the sliced onion and spring onion for about 45 seconds. Add the shrimp and fry until they change colour. Add the meat, peas and mushrooms and stir-fry for about 30 seconds. Return the egg to the wok, and add the seasonings and rice. Stir-fry over high heat until well mixed. Sprinkle over the coriander and serve.

LOTUS RICE

375 g (¾ lb) short-grain glutinous white rice, soaked
  overnight
6 dried lotus leaves, soaked
6 dried scallops, soaked
8 dried Chinese mushrooms, soaked
30 g (1 oz) dried pressed duck, soaked (optional)
30 g (1 oz) dried shrimps, soaked
45 g (1½ oz) canned bamboo shoots, drained
45 g (1½ oz) canned water chestnuts, drained
185 g (6 oz) Chinese roast pork
2 small Chinese sausages (optional)
45 g (1½ oz) roasted peanuts
4 spring onions
salt and white pepper
2 tablespoons oil

Drain the soaked ingredients and set the lotus leaves
aside. Bring a small saucepan of water to the boil and
drop in scallops, mushrooms, duck and shrimps. Cook
until softened. Drain, reserving the liquid.

Cut all into very fine dice. Dice bamboo shoots,
water chestnuts, pork and sausages finely. Mix diced
ingredients with the rice, moistening with a little of the
reserved liquid. Add peanuts, finely chopped spring
onions, salt and pepper.

Brush the inside of each lotus leaf with oil. Divide
the rice mixture between the leaves and fold up leaves
to enclose the rice. Tie bundles with string or set each
in a small heatproof glass dish, brushed with oil. Place
them in a steamer to steam for about 1¼ hours, until
the rice is tender. Serve hot.

RICE CONGEE

A creamy soup of boiled rice is a breakfast or snack dish enjoyed in many parts of China. It can be served with no more than a dash of soy sauce and a sprinkling of chopped spring onion, but is delicious with thin slices of liver, pork, beef or chicken. It is traditionally accompanied by deep fried you tiau *crullers, rather like straight doughnuts, which are cut into bite-sized pieces and floated on top.*

500 g (1 lb) white rice
salt and white pepper
100 g (3½ oz) pig's liver
100 g (3½ oz) lean pork, beef or chicken
2 eggs, beaten (optional)
3–4 *you tiau* crullers, deep-fried (optional)
45 g (1½ oz) salted turnip or other preserved
    vegetables
4 spring onions

Place the rice in a deep pot with 6 cups water. Bring to the boil and simmer until the rice is so soft that it is beginning to break up. Add more water if needed to make a reasonably thick soup. Season to taste with salt and white pepper.

Slice the liver very thinly and blanch quickly in boiling water. Slice the meat into very thin strips. Place liver and meat in deep bowls with a little beaten egg (or a whole egg, if preferred). Pour on the hot gruel.

Cut the fried *you tiau* crullers into bite-sized pieces and serve on the side with finely diced turnip or preserved vegetables and spring onions. Have light soy sauce and chilli sauce or chilli oil available for adding to taste.

DESSERTS

ALMOND JELLY WITH MIXED FRUITS

1 tablespoon gelatine
1½ cups lukewarm water
1 teaspoon almond extract, or to taste
45 g (1½ oz) sugar
¾ cup evaporated milk
canned fruit cocktail in syrup

Soften gelatine in lukewarm water and heat until dissolved. Mix in almond extract, sugar and evaporated milk and heat through, stirring to dissolve the sugar. Pour into a greased tray and leave to set.

When firm cut into diamond shaped pieces. Serve in glass dessert dishes topped with mixed fruit. Pour on a generous amount of the syrup. Serve chilled.

SWEET PEANUT SOUP

185 g (6 oz) raw peanuts
2 tablespoons white sesame seeds
8 cups water
125 g (¼ lb) white sugar
4 tablespoons cornflour
½ cup thick cream

Place peanuts in a hot oven or under a moderate grill to roast until lightly coloured. Place in a cloth and rub off skins. Toast sesame seeds lightly and grind peanuts and sesame seeds to a fine powder in a heavy-duty blender, adding a little water if needed.

Pour into a saucepan with water and sugar and simmer until smooth and creamy. Strain to remove any large pieces of peanut and bring to the boil again. Mix cornflour with thick cream and stir into the soup. Heat through until thickened. Serve warm.

RED BEAN SOUP

250 g (½ lb) small red beans
8 cups water
1 cup sugar
1 dried tangerine peel
30 g (1 oz) dried lotus buds (optional)

Place red beans with water, tangerine peel and lotus buds in a saucepan and simmer for about 2 hours until beans are completely tender. Add sugar and heat through until completely melted. Cook for a further 10 minutes on high heat. Serve warm.

Birds Nest Soup with Quail Eggs, and Sour and Hot Sichuan Soup (recipes pages 39 and 40).

TOFFEE APPLES

3 firm red apples
60 g (2 oz) cornflour
60 g (2 oz) plain flour
1 egg white
flavourless vegetable oil for deep frying
1 tablespoon sesame oil
250 g (½ lb) sugar
2 tablespoons white sesame seeds
iced water
ice cubes

Oil a serving plate lightly and have all ingredients and utensils on hand, as this dish requires precision timing.

Peel apples, remove cores and cut each into 8 pieces. Lightly beat egg and combine with water and the flours to make a smooth, thin batter. Put oil for deep frying onto heat and add sesame oil.

Mix sugar with 1 cup water and 1 tablespoon oil and bring to the boil. Simmer until it forms a thick, light coloured toffee. Test if toffee is ready by dropping a spoonful into iced water. If it hardens immediately, the toffee is done. Add sesame seeds to the toffee and set near the cooker.

When oil is almost at smoking point coat several pieces of apple with the batter and put into the oil. Fry to a golden brown. Lift out with wooden chopsticks and place in the toffee syrup. When coated transfer to the iced water to harden. Place on the oiled serving plate. Cook all apple in this way and serve immediately with the bowl of ice water. Dip into the water again to harden if the toffee has begun to soften.

Firm ripe banana may be used in this way also, either sliced or whole.

Toffee Apples (recipe page 49).

GLOSSARY

AGAR AGAR: A gelatinous seaweed, sold dried in powdered or strip form. It is used instead of gelatine for sweets, and because it sets without refrigeration it is suited to hot climates.

BAMBOO SHOOTS: Cream-coloured spear-like shoots of the bamboo plant. Fresh shoots must be peeled to the firm heart and then boiled. Also sold canned in water or in a sauce usually based on soy. Store in the refrigerator in a dish of fresh water, changing the water daily, for up to ten days. Winter bamboo shoots have a better flavour than the common variety.

BEANCURD: Soft beancurd is prepared by setting a liquid of ground soy beans with gypsum. Hard beancurd, or beancurd cake, is soft beancurd compressed to remove most of the water content.

BIRD'S NESTS: A glutinous, fibrous substance, almost transparent cream in colour, produced by a certain kind of swallow for building nests.

BOK CHOY: *see* Chinese cabbage

CHINESE BROWN VINEGAR: Fermented rice vinegar, mild but pungent. Use white vinegar or malt vinegar as a substitute.

CHINESE CABBAGE: Also known as Tientsin cabbage, celery cabbage, *nap*, and *wombok*, it has long pale-green thick stems with light-green, leaves and grows, tightly packed, up to 40 cm high. *Bok choy*, another cabbage-like vegetable known in some countries as 'Chinese cabbage', has white stems and dark-green leaves; it can be substituted for genuine Chinese cabbage in most recipes.

CHINESE RICE WINE: The pale, clear Shaoshing is most suitable for cooking, though it is not readily available. Rose Wine Spirits, if available, can be substituted, but use no more than half the quantity recommended for rice wine. Pale dry sherry is a good substitute.

CHINESE SAUSAGES: Thin dried sausages filled with pork fat and ham or cured liver. Should be steamed before use.

CHOW CHOW: *see* pickled/preserved vegetables

CLOUD EAR FUNGUS: A dark-brown, almost black, crinkly gelatinous fungus, about 3 cm in diameter, which gives a musky flavour to many Chinese dishes and is a common ingredient in vegetarian cooking. Store in an airtight container.

EGG NOODLES: Also known as *dan mien*, these are thin dried yellow noodles, either round or flat. They are sold in small bundles, which must first be soaked to soften and separate the strands.

FIVE-SPICE POWDER: A blend of star anise, fennel, aniseed, cloves and cassia (similar to cinnamon stick). The spices are roasted before grinding.

GINGER: Fresh root ginger is essential in Chinese cooking, and dried powdered ginger is *not* a substitute. Fresh ginger should be peeled or scraped to remove the thin flaky skin, and the flesh sliced, finely shredded or grated.

GINGER WINE: An infusion of shredded fresh ginger in Chinese rice wine, dry sherry or dry white wine. Leave for at least 1 hour before use.

GLUTINOUS RICE: A rice of very short grain that becomes very sticky when cooked, and is therefore also known as 'sticky' rice.

HOISIN SAUCE: A sweet brownish-red sauce made with garlic, chillies, spices and soy beans. Often labelled 'Barbecue Sauce'. Available in cans and jars, it keeps indefinitely in the refrigerator.

JELLY FISH, PROCESSED: Gelatinous dried shreds of jelly fish. Substitute pea-flour vermicelli (transparent vermicelli) or shredded agar agar.

MANGE-TOUT: Snow peas.

OYSTER SAUCE: A thick brown sauce made from oysters, soy sauce and salt. It gives a delicate, fishy flavour.

PICKLED/PRESERVED VEGETABLES: *Mei gan tsai* is a salted dried mustard cabbage used with braised meats; *tai tau tsoi* is a heavily salted preserved turnip sold in cans or by weight; and *chow chow* preserves are a mixture of fruit, ginger and vegetables used in sweet and savoury dishes. There are other types of pickled and moist-preserved cabbage and related greens that add saltiness and flavour.

RICE DOUGH ROLLS: Thin sheets of rice-flour dough, steamed, then cut into noodles. Also sold as tightly compressed rolls which can be cut crossways into noodles.

RICE-FLOUR NOODLES: Fairly thin *hor fun* cut into flat strands about 0.5 cm wide, and available fresh or dried; the dry type must be soaked for up to 30 minutes to soften.

RICE VERMICELLI: Very fine threads of *mie fun*. When deep fried they puff up quite dramatically and become very crisp.

SALTED BLACK BEANS: Preserved, fermented salted soy beans used as a well-flavoured seasoning ingredient in Chinese cooking. If unavailable, add more salt and soy sauce.

SESAME OIL: A nutty dark-brown oil made from sesame seeds. Gives a rich flavour and nutty aroma. Never used alone for deep frying, for it burns at a relatively low temperature and has too strong a taste.

SESAME SEEDS: White sesame seeds are used as a garnish for many types of sweets. High in protein.

SHARK FIN: Clear 'needles' of gelatinous shark fin are sold in packets and need to be soaked before use. Whole shark fin requires longer soaking before cooking.

SOY SAUCE: Available in light, dark and sweet types. 'Light' is a thin watery liquid, is quite salty, and is most often used in Chinese cooking. 'Dark' is used when sauces or meats need additional colour, and is usually less salty than the light type.

STAR ANISE: An eight-pointed star-shaped fragrant Chinese spice with a rich anise flavour.

TIENTSIN CABBAGE: *see* Chinese cabbage

TRANSPARENT VERMICELLI: Also known as *fun sie* or cellophane noodles, these are fine threads of glass-like dried noodles made from mung bean flour.

VERMICELLI SHEETS: Transparent sheets of mung bean flour, which can be shredded and used as a vegetable or garnish. *See also* jelly fish, processed.

WATER CHESTNUTS: Brown-skinned crisp white nuts, available fresh or canned, and used as a vegetable in Chinese cooking.

WINTER MELON: Large white-fleshed melon similar in external appearance to watermelon. Used in soups and stewed dishes. Available canned. Substitute squash.

WONTON WRAPPERS: Prepared rice-flour skins for *wonton*. Sold fresh or frozen.

YOU TIAU CRULLERS: Long straight doughnuts, deep-fried.

INDEX